NBA CHAMPION

LEBRON JAMES

BY LAURA K. MURRAY

Essential Library
An Imprint of Abdo Publishing
abdobooks.com

ABDOBOOKS.COM

Published by Abdo Publishing, a division of ABDO, PO Box 398166, Minneapolis, Minnesota 55439. Copyright © 2020 by Abdo Consulting Group, Inc. International copyrights reserved in all countries. No part of this book may be reproduced in any form without written permission from the publisher. Essential Library™ is a trademark and logo of Abdo Publishing.

Printed in the United States of America, North Mankato, Minnesota.
042019
092019

THIS BOOK CONTAINS RECYCLED MATERIALS

Cover Photo: Alex Gallardo/AP Images
Interior Photos: Ed Betz/AP Images, 4; Aynsley Floyd/AP Images, 6; Tony Dejak/AP Images, 8, 34, 37, 44, 64–65, 90; Everett Collection/Shutterstock Images, 13; Mark Duncan/AP Images, 14, 76; Threeblur0/Wikimedia, 16; J. D. Pooley/AP Images, 21; Bruce Schwartzman/AP Images, 24; Bob Falcetti/Icon SMI/Newscom, 31; Mark Goldman/Icon SMI/Newscom, 33; Stuart Ramson/AP Images, 41; Michael Conroy/AP Images, 43; Duane Burleson/AP Images, 48; Eric Gay/AP Images, 51; John Raoux/AP Images, 53; Charles Krupa/AP Images, 54; Phil Masturzo/Akron Beacon-Journal/AP Images, 56; J. Pat Carter/AP Images, 61; Tom DiPace/AP Images, 63, 66; Steve Dykes/AP Images, 70; Wilfredo Lee/AP Images, 74; Gregory Shamus/Getty Images Sport/Getty Images, 79; Eric Risberg/AP Images, 82; Alex Menendez/AP Images, 84; Tony Avelar/AP Images, 86; Charlie Ans/Splash News/Newscom, 89; Phil Long/AP Images, 94; Nell Redmond/AP Images, 97

Editor: Patrick Donnelly
Series Designer: Laura Graphenteen

LIBRARY OF CONGRESS CONTROL NUMBER: 2018967345

PUBLISHER'S CATALOGING-IN-PUBLICATION DATA

Names: Murray, Laura K., author.
Title: LeBron James: NBA champion / by Laura K. Murray
Other title: NBA champion
Description: Minneapolis, Minnesota: Abdo Publishing, 2020 | Series: Star athletes | Includes online resources and index.
Identifiers: ISBN 9781532119880 (lib. bdg.) | ISBN 9781532174711 (ebook) | ISBN 9781644940952 (pbk.)
Subjects: LCSH: James, LeBron, 1984---Juvenile literature. | Basketball players--United States--Biography--Juvenile literature. | African American basketball players--Biography--Juvenile literature. | African American professional athletes--Biography--Juvenile literature | Sports--Biography--Juvenile literature.
Classification: DDC 796.323092 [B]--dc23

CONTENTS

WELCOME TO
JAMESTOWN

It was a hot summer night on June 26, 2003, and thousands of basketball fans crowded into Gund Arena in Cleveland, Ohio. Most were decked out in the wine and gold colors of the Cavaliers, the city's team in the National Basketball Association (NBA). Some fans had waited outside for hours, holding signs featuring slogans and greetings such as "Welcome to Jamestown." Lines snaked around the block, made up of those awaiting the chance to buy the new team jersey boasting the number 23. Inside the arena, all eyes were on the jumbo screens, where the 2003 NBA Draft was about to begin. More than two million households around the country watched on television.

The action was taking place hundreds of miles away, at New York's Madison Square Garden. This year's draft had generated buzz over several

James shakes hands with NBA commissioner David Stern after he was announced as the Cavaliers' pick.

In early June 2003, James spoke to the media about the upcoming draft.

promising players. But to Cavaliers fans and many others, one name stood out above all the rest: LeBron James.

Just 18 years old, the six-foot-eight, 240-pound high school phenom sat at a table in a custom-made white suit, awaiting his name to be called as the first overall draft pick. James was one of the most anticipated draft picks in NBA history after becoming a nationally known high school star who carried the nickname "King James."

James was a great all-around player with keen passing abilities, top-notch ball-handling skills, and extraordinary athleticism that allowed him to explode to the hoop. He was also versatile, able to play all positions. Coaches liked his team-focused work ethic and unselfish play. The media gravitated toward his outgoing personality and superstar image. He was only the second player ever to be the first overall pick straight out of high school. The first had been Georgia's Kwame Brown, who had been selected by the Washington Wizards in 2001.

Many saw James as the saving grace for the Cavaliers—and for the city of Cleveland, whose professional sports teams were said to be cursed. The sagging Cavs team had hit rock bottom the previous season, tying with the Denver Nuggets for the league's worst record at 17–65. The team lacked discipline and leadership, and game attendance had dwindled, causing some

FIRST PICKS

Those who were skeptical of LeBron James's chances of enjoying quick prep-to-pro success had plenty of examples of failed number one picks to back them up. Kwame Brown was drafted number one straight out of high school. However, like many other first picks, he didn't live up to the expectations. In 2006, the NBA changed its rules, now requiring that players entering the draft be 19 years old and that one season have passed since their high school graduation.

LeBron James holds his jersey after being introduced to the media as a Cleveland Cavalier in 2003.

sportscasters to compare the Cavs' generally empty arena to a ghost town. To many, there was nowhere to go but up. When Cleveland drew the number one draft pick in May 2003, there had been no question of whom they would select.

A KING IS BORN

To Cleveland fans, James was more than the number one pick. He was also a hometown hero, having grown up about 40 miles (64 km) away from Cleveland, in Akron, Ohio. He had been named Ohio's Mr. Basketball three times and led his high school team to three state championships. As a junior, he appeared on the cover of *Sports Illustrated*. Now, with the hopes of so many pinned on him, James had a lot to prove.

"Cleveland always has the rug pulled out from under it," ABC-TV host Mike Tirico said. "Tonight, it's a Cleveland night to celebrate sports. One of Ohio's own . . . comes to a team of their own."[1]

NBA commissioner David Stern took the stage to begin the draft. The Cavaliers had five minutes to announce their pick. A few minutes later, Stern returned to announce that the Cavs had officially selected LeBron James. The newest

THE CLEVELAND CURSE

For many Cleveland fans, LeBron James was the answer to a long-standing curse they believed kept the city's major league teams from winning a championship. Besides the Cavaliers, Cleveland is home to the Indians of Major League Baseball (MLB) and the Browns of the National Football League (NFL). When James signed with the Cavs in 2003, no Cleveland sports team had won a championship since 1964, the year the Browns won the Super Bowl. The city's long-suffering fan bases had experienced disappointment after disappointment, from agonizing losses to dashed hopes, which fueled talk of the curse.

Cavalier donned a team cap, hugging his agent and then his mother, Gloria, before making his way to the stage to accept his team jersey. There were cheers in the crowd, but also boos and chants of "Overrated!"

"At whatever position I'll play, I'll bring the willingness to win because I don't accept losing very well."[3]
— LeBron James, 2003

The decision to select James was not a surprise, but that didn't put a damper on the celebrations back in Cleveland. Gund Arena erupted in cheers, music, and dancing, with balloons and confetti dropping from the ceiling. Citing James's childhood growing up with a single mother, one ESPN commentator called it "a great American story, from tough times to tremendous success."[2]

The 18-year-old stood to make millions in endorsements as a professional athlete. But the pressure was on to prove himself. He was already being compared with not only modern-day NBA stars such as Kobe Bryant and Kevin Garnett but also all-time greats such as Larry Bird, Magic Johnson, and Michael Jordan. While some believed that James would never live up to the hype, others took a more moderate stance, cautioning that rookies usually need a few years in the league before finding their groove. ESPN.com's Marc Stein predicted, "A rough rookie indoctrination . . . is almost guaranteed." James himself said, "I know I'm a marked man."[4] No one knew for sure whether he would achieve the greatness of superstardom or fizzle out without fulfilling his potential.

A PLAYER FOR THE AGES

TALENTED ROOKIES

The 2003 NBA Draft is remembered for its depth of talented players. Besides LeBron James, it produced a significant number of future NBA stars, including Carmelo Anthony (third overall, Denver Nuggets), Chris Bosh (fourth overall, Toronto Raptors), and Dwyane Wade (fifth overall, Miami Heat). These players are often credited with transforming their franchises and the league in general. Another memorable aspect of the draft was its pool of high schoolers. A record nine high school seniors were selected in the first round.

Since his entrance into the NBA in 2003, LeBron James has carved out a place as one of the greatest basketball players not just of his generation but of all time. In an NBA career that has spanned more than 15 years, James has continued to dominate, racking up eye-popping stats and achievements. Through the 2017–18 season, he had been named the NBA's Most Valuable Player (MVP) four times and the NBA Finals MVP three times. He had played in 14 All-Star games, won three NBA championships, and brought home two Olympic gold medals. Even in his fifteenth season, James posted career-best numbers

TAKE HIM TO THE BANK

In 2003, the NBA was in a recession. That year, legendary Michael Jordan had retired (for the third and final time), and the Finals had been the least watched ever. The lackluster response was blamed on the league's drought of "bankable" stars, apart from Kobe Bryant and Shaquille O'Neal of the Los Angeles Lakers. The league was eager for more star players who could galvanize fans across the country to get excited about the games—and buy tickets and merchandise. Enter the 2003 draft class, which included an exciting crop of names, including teenage standout LeBron James.

in rebounds and assists per game. Along the way, James has become one of the world's highest-paid athletes, securing landmark endorsement deals in addition to his contract payments.

James's path into the record books has not always been smooth. At various points, he has been called the world's most liked and most disliked athlete, generating controversy on and off the court. Most notably, his 2010 decision to leave his hometown team as a free agent and sign with the Miami Heat—announced in a live television event— went down in sports history as a public relations disaster and gave fuel to his loudest critics.

Nothing about James is small, from his physical stature to his moves on the court to his personality. He has attracted both public support and criticism for voicing his opinions on politics and issues such as racism. Meanwhile, he has shown he is more than a basketball player,

James has transcended his sport to become one of the most famous people in the world.

proving himself to be savvy in business as well. He has found success in the entertainment industry, starting his own production company as well as hosting shows and appearing in movies. He has also made headlines with his charitable work, often calling attention to his own humble beginnings growing up without a permanent home for many of his childhood years. Through it all, James has never lost focus on his quest for greatness.

STRUGGLES AND **SUCCESSES**

LeBron Raymone James was born December 30, 1984, in Akron, Ohio. His mother, Gloria, was just 16 years old at the time. James's father was never part of his life, so LeBron and Gloria relied on each other, forming a tight-knit bond through the years as they struggled to make ends meet. For the first three years of LeBron's life, the two lived with Gloria's family in a four-bedroom Victorian home in Akron's Boondocks neighborhood. Four generations of the family lived in the house on Hickory Street, including LeBron's young uncles, Terry and Curt, his grandmother Freda, and his great-grandmother "Big Ma." Freda, a strong-willed, compassionate woman, led the household and welcomed those who needed help, even while struggling to pay her own mortgage.

LeBron James has always been a fiery competitor, even as a high school player.

LeBron grew up in Akron, an industrial city that had fallen on hard times.

Adamant that she would complete her education, Gloria went back to school and earned her high school diploma while Freda watched LeBron during the day. In 1987, Big Ma died. Then, on Christmas Day of that year, Freda died of a heart attack at 42 years old. Freda's death was a blow to the entire family. Just three years old at the time, LeBron had no idea of the turmoil his mom and uncles were experiencing. Instead, he delighted in his new toy basketball hoop, a gift from Gloria, as he ran and dunked in it over and over again.

When Gloria and her brothers could not afford to pay the bills piling up for the old house, their heat was shut off. Seeing their unsafe living conditions, a neighbor invited LeBron and Gloria to sleep on her couch. They stayed for several months. James played basketball with the neighborhood boys on a hoop made of a milk crate nailed to a telephone pole. The Jameses were eventually evicted from their family home, and the house was torn down.

Over the next several years, LeBron and his mother moved often, staying with family or friends or hopping from apartment to apartment in various Akron housing

GLORIA JAMES

LeBron's number one fan has always been his mother, Gloria, who is known for being a vocal and enthusiastic spectator of her son, "Bron Bron." She has occasionally faced criticism from the media, particularly after brushes with the law, but LeBron has always stood up for her, crediting her with ensuring their survival throughout his childhood. According to LeBron, seeing Gloria work to build a life for the two of them is a defining part of who he is. "She put me first," he said. "I knew that no matter what happened, nothing and nobody was more important to her than I was. I went without a lot of things, but never for one second did I feel unimportant or unloved."[1] Gloria's name is inked on his right bicep above his lion head tattoo.

projects. "My mom would always say, 'Don't get too comfortable, because we may not be here long,'" James later remembered.[2] At one point, they moved 12 times in three years. They lived on welfare and food stamps, and LeBron was left alone as Gloria worked nights. "Sometimes I went to bed not knowing if I was going to see her in the morning," he recalled. "I became afraid that one day I would wake up, and she would be gone forever."[3] All they had was each other.

INTRO TO SPORTS

By the time LeBron was in fourth grade, his unstable home life showed in his grades. He was somewhat awkward and shy, and because he was constantly moving and starting new schools, he found it difficult to make friends. Unsure of what each new day would bring, he did not always know which school to go to or how to get there. He missed nearly 100 days of school in fourth grade, often choosing to stay home and play video games instead.[4]

Still, he stayed out of trouble and off the streets, avoiding the drugs and gang activity that permeated his neighborhoods.

In 1993, youth football coach Bruce Kelker, a family friend, came to LeBron's housing project to recruit players for his East Dragons rec team. LeBron was outside playing with other kids and informed Kelker that football was his favorite sport. Kelker had the kids race each other, declaring that he would make the winner his running back. A natural athlete and both big and fast for his age, LeBron won handily. He hadn't played organized sports before but was excited to be on the team. On his first handoff, LeBron ran 80 yards for a touchdown.[6] Kelker knew he had a star on his hands.

Football proved to be a turning point in LeBron's life, giving him focus, stability, and his first experiences with sportsmanship—and success. He scored 17 touchdowns in six games.[7] Meanwhile, Gloria helped at practices

FATHER FIGURES

Throughout his life, LeBron has had several coaches, mentors, and family friends whom he credits as important father figures to him. There has been plenty of speculation over the years as to the identity of LeBron's biological father. When LeBron became a father himself, he vowed that he would have a different relationship with his own children. "That's my main goal, to try and be a better father than the one I had," he posted on his Instagram account. "I didn't know him. I didn't know the situation he was in. But I'm going to do my job the best way I can."[8]

TAKING TO THE FIELD

Before he was a basketball superstar, LeBron dreamed of playing in the NFL—and many believe he could have. His football coaches say he applied the same champion traits to football as he did to basketball, including an incredible knowledge of the game and a refuse-to-lose attitude to go along with his size and speed. He was an all-state wide receiver his sophomore and junior years and found his way into his high school's record books. Before his senior year, LeBron gave up football after injuring his wrist during summer basketball.

in place of paying the team fees. They both found a sense of belonging in the sports community. Kelker made sure LeBron got to practice and invited LeBron and Gloria to live temporarily in his small apartment with him and his girlfriend, acting as a mentor to LeBron and a dependable presence in the boy's life. For his part, LeBron loved football and started to dream of playing in the NFL. However, other parents thought the team was lying about LeBron's age and demanded to see his birth certificate. When an embarrassed LeBron began hunching to hide his size, Kelker told him to stand tall and proud: "You ain't ever going to blend in. And that can be a good thing."[9]

LeBron always had his mother, Gloria, in his corner.

AT HOME WITH THE WALKERS

In late 1993, LeBron and Gloria left Kelker's apartment, and Gloria wondered whether she should send LeBron away to live with other relatives. Another football coach, Frank Walker, whose son Frankie Jr. was LeBron's friend and football teammate, offered to take in LeBron for a time. Gloria, hesitant at first, allowed her son to live with the Walker family while she saved money so she and LeBron could afford a permanent place of their own.

"I know my background, know what my mother went through. I never get too high on my stardom or what I can do."[10]

— LeBron James

LeBron lived with Frank and Pam Walker and their three children for a year and a half. He showed a penchant for fitting in with new people and picking up on routines quickly. He was expected to go to school, do chores, and finish his homework. For the first time in his life, LeBron learned discipline, structure, and responsibility. Later in his life, LeBron considered living with the Walkers his first experience with "a real family," adding, "It opened my eyes up to become what I am today, why I act the way I am today."[11] LeBron still saw his mother on weekends and remained close with her. With this new structure to his life, he didn't miss any more school, and his grades improved, with music, art, and gym being his favorite classes. He would soon discover another favorite that would change the course of his life—basketball.

LIKE MIKE

LeBron began wearing the number 23 in high school as a nod to Michael Jordan, whom many consider the greatest player in NBA history. Jordan wore 23 for much of his career. When LeBron got his own room, he covered its walls with Jordan posters and Nike ads. In 2001, 16-year-old LeBron met his hero after Jordan came to see him play. LeBron recalled, "It was like meeting God for the first time."[12] As LeBron has surpassed several of Jordan's records, lively debates center on which of them may be, in fact, the greatest of all time.

A SHOOTING STAR

Frank Walker introduced nine-year-old LeBron James to basketball basics, teaching him how to dribble and shoot left-handed. Playing on the makeshift dirt basketball court in the Walkers' backyard, LeBron played for hours, with Frank preaching the fundamentals of the game but making sure homework came first. LeBron proved to be a quick study who improved so quickly that Frank soon made him an assistant coach to the eight-year-olds. Frank was one of several men who remained an important father figure to LeBron throughout his life. In sixth grade, LeBron reunited with Gloria, moving into a rent-controlled, two-bedroom apartment in the Spring Hill complex, where they would remain for several years. LeBron still saw the Walkers often, since they had become like family to each other.

CHAPTER THREE

LeBron James shows his moves in warm-ups during his senior year of high school.

Another lifelong mentor entered LeBron's life in 1995 when he caught the attention of youth basketball coach Dru Joyce II. After Joyce saw LeBron playing basketball at Akron's Summit Lake Community Center, he contacted Gloria and convinced her to let LeBron play on his Amateur Athletic Union (AAU) team, the Shooting Stars. LeBron liked the idea of playing with other kids and traveling to places he had never been—even to Cleveland, just a half hour away.

The Shooting Stars practiced in a small gym with a linoleum floor. Coach Joyce noticed that ten-year-old LeBron showed unique potential from the day he first stepped onto the court, later calling LeBron "a sponge" who soaked up everything coaches taught him. Even into LeBron's adulthood, coaches would remark on his unique ability and hunger to improve. The Shooting Stars played so well that they earned a spot in the national AAU tournament in Cocoa Beach, Florida, for age 11 and under. They finished ninth out of 64 teams, no small feat for a bunch of kids from Akron. They began dreaming about what they could accomplish next.

The teammates formed close friendships. LeBron and his buddies Dru Joyce III ("Little Dru"), Willie McGee, and Sian Cotton were labeled "the Fab Four" by a reporter. LeBron would consider them brothers for the rest of his life. The friends kept dreaming big together, finding success in subsequent years as they won national championships and became the pride of Akron. The Fab Four made sure to have fun while they were playing—and to them, fun meant winning.

"We were raised that you gotta win. It was just survival," said LeBron. "But it was *always* fun."[2] LeBron, six feet tall and lanky as an eighth grader, had raw natural talent, pushed to the forefront with his relentless pursuit of making himself and his team the best. He put in the hours practicing, and he wasn't a ball hog. On top of everything, he possessed an uncanny full-floor vision, seeing opportunities for passes or cuts and reading opponents' moves before they happened.

HIGH SCHOOL HIGHLIGHTS

The Fab Four agreed they would all attend the same high school to continue playing together. They decided

AN EARLY DECISION

Of the original Fab Four, it was Little Dru who decided he wanted to attend St. V rather than the public high school. This was a surprise to the rest of the group, but Little Dru believed the coaches at Buchtel wouldn't play him because of his small size, and he wanted to follow Coach Keith Dambrot. After discussion, the other three made up their minds to go too.

on St. Vincent–St. Mary High School, or "St. V," a private Catholic school with a mostly white student population and known more for academics than sports. Playing for St. V's "Fighting Irish," the Fab Four were on the receiving end of backlash, as some in the black community viewed it as a betrayal and resented the players for choosing the private school over Buchtel, the public school with a predominantly minority student body. It was an adjustment for LeBron, who recalled, "I had never hung around white people in my life, and I just didn't know how to get along with them. I didn't know what to say."[3]

Sports helped to bridge that gap. The boys played for Keith Dambrot, a former college coach who soon chose Coach Joyce as an assistant coach. It didn't take long for the team to jell. Already known as "King James," LeBron posted 15 points and eight rebounds in his first high school game in 1999. The wins kept coming, with LeBron averaging 18 points per game during his freshman year. The undefeated Irish captured the Division III state title in 2000, bolstered by LeBron's 25 points in the championship game.

With the arrival of LeBron's middle school teammate Romeo Travis at St. V, the Fab Four eventually became the Fab Five. St. V won its second straight state title in 2001, playing before a record crowd of 17,612 in Columbus, Ohio. Sophomore LeBron had begun to make headlines as an unbelievable talent, attracting the attention of scouts, recruiters, and the media. Among other honors, he found himself on *USA Today*'s All-USA First Team, the first sophomore ever selected. He would retain his spot the following two years. The Irish had a 53–1 record throughout LeBron's freshman and sophomore years. LeBron and his teammates played with aggression, focus, and skill. As always, Gloria cheered madly from the stands.

OPENING THE FLOODGATES

The growing fame was a lot to handle. Speculation began to swirl that LeBron would head to the NBA straight from high school. Fans chanted his name

IN THE CLASSROOM

At school, LeBron was well liked by teachers and students, applying the same work ethic that he brought to the court into the classroom and eventually raising his grade point average (GPA) from about 2.8 to above 3.0 his senior year.[4] He viewed school as a sanctuary of sorts, as school officials barred media from the property during the school day. His favorite subject in high school was English.

> *"We shared everything with one another, and it became a kind of unspoken rule: if you're eating something, everybody gets a piece, pizza, Starbursts, Twizzlers—it didn't matter. All for one and one for all."[7]*
>
> — LeBron on the Fab Four

'BRON AND 'MELO

In high school, LeBron crossed paths with another 2003 NBA Draft pick: Carmelo Anthony. The two met at a basketball camp before playing each other in high school, LeBron at St. V and Carmelo at Oak Hill Academy. In a notable 2002 showcase, the high school stars were matched up in front of more than 11,000 people in Trenton, New Jersey. Oak Hill won. The two stars stayed good friends throughout their NBA careers, forging a bond over their similar upbringings and love of the game.

as he dunked over the heads of his opponents. Players from the opposing team asked for his autograph. People were scalping tickets to his games. His teammates and coaches, however, went a long way in preventing him from getting too cocky. "You don't even play defense," Coach Dambrot scoffed after hearing that LeBron was being labeled as the best sophomore in the nation.[5]

Then things got rocky. Junior year was, in LeBron's words, "a major disaster."[6] The shake-up began with Coach Dambrot's departure before the season began. Coach Joyce replaced him as head coach. But the team didn't give him their respect or focus, still fixated on the coach they had lost. Their

LeBron works on his game at a basketball camp in the summer before his junior year.

play was off, as they pulled out ugly wins and suffered uglier losses.

In February 2002, a now six-foot-seven LeBron appeared on the cover of *Sports Illustrated* with the words

NATIONAL TV

In December 2002, more than 11,000 fans crowded into a Cleveland arena for St. V's game against rival Oak Hill. ESPN2 was taking the unusual step of broadcasting a high school basketball game nationally. Reporters from *USA Today* and the *New York Times* also covered the game. After playing to the crowd during warm-ups, LeBron seemed to have let the pressure get to him to start the game, coming out cold and missing his first shots. But then he relaxed and awed the crowd, finishing with 31 points, 13 rebounds, and six assists. One of his dunks was featured prominently on ESPN's *SportsCenter*. Joined by NBA Hall of Famer Bill Walton, sportscaster Dick Vitale declared, "He's the truth, the whole truth, and nothing but the truth."[9]

"The Chosen One." The cover opened up the floodgates to national fame. High demand for tickets meant that St. V's games had been moved to the Rhodes Arena at the University of Akron. The crazed media attention distracted the team from basketball, and, despite their coach's warnings, they began acting like rock stars rather than high schoolers, sometimes staying up until the early morning hours before games. "We had become big-headed jerks, me in particular," James later said, "and we are to blame for that, but so are adults who treated us that way and then sat back and smugly watched the self-destruction."[8]

In the state championship the following month, the unthinkable happened: St. V lost. The team took the loss hard. Still, LeBron was named State Player of the Year for the second time and also Gatorade Player of the Year.

While in high school, LeBron was interviewed at the Jordan Brand Classic, a national high school all-star game held in Washington, DC.

But for LeBron, everything had become clear: senior year needed to be different—and St. V was going to win the national championship.

THE BIG TIME

St. Vincent–St. Mary bounced back during LeBron James's senior year. The team was determined not to lose sight of the championship this time, even though the hype surrounding LeBron was at full force. Even scrimmages brought swarms of media and required police presence. LeBron appeared on the cover of *ESPN the Magazine* and fielded calls from *Good Morning America* and *The Oprah Winfrey Show*. To close out LeBron's high school career, the Irish took back the state championship. The win put them in first place in the *USA Today* national poll, which gave them the mythical national championship. LeBron became the first player to be named Ohio's Mr. Basketball for a third time.

Meanwhile, fame was brewing controversy. In a 2002 incident dubbed "Hummergate," Gloria bought LeBron an expensive Hummer sport-utility vehicle for his eighteenth birthday. Then came the investigation by the Ohio High School Athletic

LeBron James shoots over Indiana's Ron Artest in December 2003.

CASHING IN

By LeBron's senior year, St. V was nationally competitive and sold out arenas around the country. Some criticized adults for making money off LeBron and then punishing him for incidents such as Jerseygate. "What the media has done in a sense is build this kid to a level that was impossible to live up to," said Coach Dru Joyce. "He never said he was the greatest high school player ever. You guys built him up. Now everybody wants to knock him down."[1]

Association (OHSAA). Days after LeBron was cleared from Hummergate, an incident known as "Jerseygate" took place. After LeBron accepted two sports jerseys from a Cleveland store, the OHSAA declared LeBron ineligible to play in any remaining games. The suspension was later shortened to two games, but LeBron and his coaches felt they were being targeted unfairly.

In late April 2003, LeBron surprised no one by announcing that he would go pro and make himself available for the NBA Draft. The draft lottery took place on May 22. But LeBron had another deal to take care of late the night before: deciding on a shoe endorsement deal. The 18-year-old chose Nike over Reebok, signing a seven-year, $90 million contract.

Excitement grew throughout Ohio when the Cleveland Cavaliers won the rights to the number one pick in the draft lottery. The following month, the Cavaliers officially selected LeBron with that pick and signed him

LeBron stands in front of his controversial Hummer that almost cost him his eligibility during his senior season.

to a standard three-year rookie contract worth a total of $12.96 million. With endorsement deals totaling more than $100 million, it was an unbelievable rise from where he and his mother had started. Now, once again, it was time to prove himself. "I can handle it," LeBron would repeat when asked about the immense pressure.[2] But many had a

HUMMERGATE

In 2002, LeBron rolled through Akron in what would become an infamous silver Hummer H2 SUV, valued at well over $50,000. It included a DVD player, three TVs, a PlayStation 2, and "King James" logos. The financing of the flashy vehicle raised questions because Gloria James was unemployed and on welfare. It was a red flag for the Ohio High School Athletic Association (OHSAA), whose rules stated that a high school athlete could not capitalize on athletic fame by receiving money or gifts. After an investigation, the OHSAA cleared LeBron, finding no evidence that he had received the vehicle from an outside source. Gloria had obtained a loan for the car by borrowing against what LeBron was expected to make when he turned professional.

difficult time believing that the teenager understood what he was getting himself into.

LIVING UP TO THE HYPE

On October 29, 2003, 18-year-old LeBron James made his NBA regular-season debut with the Cavaliers against the Sacramento Kings. More than 17,000 fans crowded into Sacramento's ARCO Arena to witness the historic moment. The normally stoic James couldn't sleep the night before. "Everyone was waiting to see what I was going to do," he later recalled.[3] For the cameras, however, he remained unmoved, saying, "There's no pressure at all. I've been getting pressure since I was 10 years old."[4]

Reporters and cameras crowded the court and locker room. Big names arrived to watch the high school phenom, including NFL wide receiver Terrell Owens and former NBA star Moses Malone. The Cavs fell 106–92, but James made it a debut for the history books, introducing himself by scoring 25 points, grabbing six rebounds, and dishing out nine assists in his 42 minutes. "When we first entered the arena, nobody knew exactly what LeBron was going to do," said Cavs coach Paul Silas. "I thought he was going to be good, but not nearly as good as he was. It was unbelievable."[5]

Some skeptics had been converted, but James kept focused on what had always mattered most: making his team the best. By January 2004, the now 19-year-old was getting more comfortable with his role on the team. He knew he had a target on his back, not only from his opponents but also from his teammates, who wanted to make sure the hyped-up rookie was put through his paces. According to James, he was ready for it. "I'm not afraid of nothing," he said.[6] It was a change from high school, but he stayed focused, thriving on the challenge and hard-fought battles of the league.

A DEBUT TO REMEMBER

LeBron's debut performance was even more impressive when put in the context of the NBA debuts of other players. ESPN pointed out that he scored more points in his first NBA game than Kwame Brown (2), Kobe Bryant (0), Eddy Curry (2), Tyson Chandler (1), Kevin Garnett (8), Tracy McGrady (0), and Jermaine O'Neal (2) combined.[7]

At the close of the 2003–04 season, James was named the NBA Rookie of the Year, averaging 20.9 points, 5.5 rebounds, and 5.9 assists per game. The Cavs finished 35–47, winning 18 more games than they had the previous season, but they were still far short of making the playoffs. As a player, James knew he had work to do—for starters, his defense needed shoring up and his jump shot needed more accuracy. But true to form, the kid from Akron was willing to put in the hours to improve in any way he could.

RISING STAR

The playoffs remained elusive the following season, despite the Cavs improving to 42–40 and James rapidly improving his own averages to 27.2 points, 7.4 rebounds, and 7.2 assists per game.[8] "I have never seen a player learn so much in one year," Silas said.[9] James was named to his first NBA All-Star Game, helping the Eastern Conference

James looks at his Rookie of the Year award.

to victory in February 2005. He would earn a spot in the All-Star Game each of the following seasons through 2018.

James continued to keep his private life guarded from public scrutiny. Despite the worldwide fame, he was still a young guy who played video games and listed cereal as his favorite meal. In October 2004, James had a big life change, welcoming a son named LeBron Jr. with girlfriend Savannah Brinson. The two had begun dating a couple of years earlier.

Throughout his rise to the top of the sports world, James had not forgotten about the Ohio community that had supported him and his mother—and he was working on paying it forward. In 2004, he started the LeBron James Family Foundation, which was focused on positively affecting children and young adults through education and initiatives. He also donated supplies to Akron schools and funds to improve the city's community centers and basketball courts.

James added another impressive entry to his bio in

A BRONZE IN ATHENS

The 2004 Summer Olympic Games were the first time the USA men's basketball team had not won gold since NBA players were first allowed to play in the Games back in 1992. Overall the team was criticized for not taking the Olympics seriously and, in some cases, acting like prima donnas. Rather than voice public disappointment about his lack of playing time, James later said he appreciated the opportunity to learn from veteran players.

James, far left, his teammates, and coach Larry Brown, center, look on in disbelief as Team USA loses to Lithuania at the 2004 Olympics.

2004: Olympian. Playing in the 2004 Summer Games in Athens, Greece, the USA men's basketball team included the likes of Tim Duncan, Allen Iverson, Dwyane Wade, and Carmelo Anthony. The team came away with a bronze medal—a disappointing finish considering the high expectations pinned on them. James, along with other rookies, spent most of the time on the bench.

THE PLAYOFFS, FINALLY

In the 2005–06 season, the Cleveland Cavaliers improved to 50–32. James hit a career milestone of 5,000 points on January 21, 2006, scoring 51 points in a Cavs win over the Utah Jazz. LeBron was named the Most Valuable Player (MVP) of the All-Star Game. Finally, the Cavs made the playoffs, the first time for the franchise since 1998, and fans rejoiced. In the first round, they powered past the Washington Wizards four games to two. Next up, they faced the favored Detroit Pistons. After dropping the first two games of the series, the Cavs fought back to take a 3–2 series lead but lost the last two games on their way to elimination. The championship remained out of reach.

In 2006, James signed a three-year, $60 million extension to his contract that would allow him to become a free agent in 2010. He was also assuming more control over his own business prospects.

LeBron James made his playoff debut against the Washington Wizards in 2006.

MAVERICK CARTER

A fellow St. V graduate, Maverick Carter is one of James's best friends and his longtime business partner. The two played together to win the high school state championship when LeBron was a freshman and Carter a senior. Referred to as "the power behind King James's throne," Carter has been alongside James his entire career, helping to build an empire of not only wealth but also power and influence.[1] Carter formerly worked at Nike representing James. As of 2019, he was the CEO of companies within LRMR Ventures, a holding company for himself, James, Rich Paul, and Randy Mims.

With his business partners, he established his own marketing firm, LRMR Marketing, which took its initials from LeBron and his childhood friends Randy Mims, Maverick Carter, and Richard Paul.

In the 2006–07 season, the Cavs again made the playoffs, with another regular-season record of 50–32. The Cavs made quick work of the Wizards and the New Jersey Nets to reach the 2007 Eastern Conference Finals. There, the Cavs had a chance at redemption as they again faced the Detroit Pistons. Unfortunately for Cavs fans, it was déjà vu, with Cleveland losing the first two games. James took over the next two games, coming up just short of a triple-double in each game as the Cavs won both to tie up the series.

Everything changed in Game 5, however, as 22-year-old James gave a legendary performance on Detroit's home court. The Cavs led 79–78 with 6:05 remaining in the game. From that point forward, James scored 29 of the Cavs' final 30 points, drilling off-balance jumpers, driving for flying dunks, and seemingly scoring at will. He finished with 48 points, and Cleveland pulled out a 109–107 win.

The Pistons were left stunned. "We threw everything we had at him," Detroit guard Chauncey Billups said afterward. "We just couldn't stop him."[2] According to James, "I was exhausted. I had nothing left. I left everything out on the floor."[3] The Cavs won the next game to take the series 4–2. Finally, they were headed to the NBA Finals.

GETTING POLITICAL

In 2007, James learned the challenge of staying apolitical. That year, he made headlines for not signing a teammate's open letter condemning the genocide in Darfur. Much of the media took the absence of his signature as apathy, although in his support the *Chicago Tribune* remarked, "It must have surprised LeBron James to hear that he has the power to stop the slaughter of thousands of people half a world away."[4] James later explained that a lack of information kept him from signing the letter and that he had since spent time educating himself. In the ensuing years, James has embraced a role of voicing his opinion on political and social issues that matter to him.

KEEPS GETTING BETTER

In the Finals, Cleveland faced the San Antonio Spurs, led by the talented trio of Tim Duncan, Tony Parker, and Manu Ginóbili. They led the Spurs to victories in each of the first three games. Meanwhile, another big life event was happening. Shortly after midnight on June 14, 2007,

the day of Game 4, LeBron and Savannah's second child, a son named Bryce Maximus James, was born. The middle name was in reference to a character in James's favorite movie, *Gladiator*. To James, the birth helped put everything in perspective. "Win, lose or draw, this is special for my family. . . . It doesn't get any better than this."[5] The Spurs completed their sweep in Game 4, but the Cavaliers had taken another step closer to championship glory.

James was warming up off the court as well and was becoming more confident in media roles. In 2007, he hosted *Saturday Night Live*. He also cohosted the ESPY awards alongside comedian Jimmy Kimmel. The following year, James produced a documentary about his life called *More Than a Game*. He was also becoming more vocal about politics as well, donating to the 2008 presidential campaign of Barack Obama and speaking out on human

LIVE FROM NEW YORK

On September 29, 2007, James hosted the season premiere of *Saturday Night Live*, which featured musical guest Kanye West. For the opening monologue (or "LeBronologue," as it was billed), James parodied his own Nike commercial and poked fun at himself and the Cavs for getting swept in the NBA Finals. In one memorable skit, he dressed in gold spandex and danced to 1980s music hits.

The Detroit Pistons had no answer for James in Game 5 of the 2007 Eastern Conference Finals.

COVER STORY

In April 2008, James became the first African American man to appear on the cover of prominent fashion magazine *Vogue*, appearing alongside Brazilian model Gisele Bündchen. The cover generated controversy, as many believed it played into racial stereotypes of African American men. In the photo, James dribbles a basketball and has a snarling expression, while his left arm is wrapped around a smiling Bündchen. Although defenders held that critics were being overly politically correct, the cover had an uncanny resemblance to historic portrayals of King Kong. *Vogue* denied any intentional parallels. For his part, James liked the cover, saying, "Who cares what anyone says?"[6]

rights issues as he educated himself on global events.

James put in the work in the off-season, sticking to rigorous workouts and getting back to shooting fundamentals under the training of coach Chris Jent. It paid off in the 2007–08 season, when James again earned MVP honors in the All-Star Game. On February 27, 2008, James became the youngest player ever to reach 10,000 career points. He was just 23 years old. Less than a month later, in a March 21 game against the Toronto Raptors, he became the Cavs' all-time leading scorer with 10,391 points. He ended the season as the league's top scorer. Now a consistent playoff contender, the Cavs again trounced the Wizards in the first round before falling to the Boston Celtics in seven games in the second round.

From left, *Chris Bosh, Dwight Howard, James, and Carlos Boozer show off their gold medals at the 2008 Olympics in Beijing, China.*

GOING, GOING . . .

In the summer of 2008, James won his first Olympic gold medal as the USA Men's Basketball team swept the competition in Beijing, China. The success continued into the 2008–09 NBA season as the Cavs had a record year, going 66–16 for a franchise record. James won his first NBA MVP Award, the first Cavaliers player to do so, averaging 28.4 points, 7.6 rebounds, 7.2 assists, 1.7 steals, and 1.2 blocks per game. He was also named the NBA Defensive Player of the Year. His MVP award ceremony took place at the St. V gym.

The Cavs faced the Orlando Magic in the Eastern Conference Finals after sweeping both the Detroit Pistons and the Atlanta Hawks. Although James posted career-best playoff numbers, averaging 35.3 points per postseason game, the Magic prevailed in six games. Following the Game 6 loss, James caught criticism for unsportsmanlike behavior when he walked off the court without shaking hands with Orlando players and refusing to speak to the media. "It's hard for me to congratulate somebody after you just lose to them," he said.[7]

> "Some of the people just wanted him to fail, and he challenged that energy, he challenged that effort. He wanted to say 'I'm great.'"[8]
>
> — Kevin Ollie, Cleveland Cavaliers teammate

In the 2009–10 season, LeBron showed his versatility as he was temporarily switched to the point guard position after several Cleveland players suffered injuries. The Cavs had the best record in the league, 61–21. Averaging 29.7 points, 7.3 rebounds, 8.6 assists, 1.0 blocks,

James walks off the court without congratulating his opponents after the Magic eliminated the Cavaliers from the 2009 NBA playoffs.

James's frustration continued to mount as the Cavaliers once again faced an early exit from the playoffs against Boston in 2010.

and 1.6 steals per game, James earned the league MVP award for the second year in a row. But the playoffs were a source of frustration again. After beating the Chicago Bulls in five games, the Cavs were eliminated by the Boston Celtics in the second round of playoffs, four games to two. The Cavs suffered one of the biggest losses in franchise history in Game 5, 120–88, with James making just three of 14 shots and eliciting choruses of boos from the Cleveland crowd.

That summer proved to be a pivotal one for James's fans in many ways. On the plus side, they could hear straight from the superstar as never before, thanks to the growing popularity of social media. On July 6, 2010, he sent his first tweet under the Twitter moniker @KingJames, encouraged by his friend Chris Paul, then of the New Orleans Hornets: "Hello World, the Real King James is in the Building 'Finally'. My Brother @oneandonlycp3 [Chris Paul] gas'd me up to jump on board so I'm here. Haaaa."[9] In a matter of seven hours, he gained more than 150,000 followers.[10]

Just a few days later, an even bigger bombshell rocked the NBA and Cavaliers fans in particular. After seven seasons as Ohio's hometown hero, James still did not have what he strived for most—an NBA championship to his name. He had big plans in mind, and they involved moving south.

THE DECISION

At 12:01 a.m. on July 1, 2010, James became an unrestricted free agent. A number of teams vied for the chance to court the six-time All-Star, and James held meetings with the Los Angeles Lakers, Los Angeles Clippers, Chicago Bulls, New Jersey Nets, and Miami Heat, in addition to the Cavs. Even President Barack Obama weighed in on the decision, suggesting in an interview that James would be a good fit for Obama's hometown Bulls.

According to James, what solidified his decision was advice from his mother, Gloria, who told him to do what would make him happy and what would be best for him. In James's mind, what would be best for him was to win a championship—it was the reason he played, after all. However, the way he revealed his choice would come to be regarded as one of the most controversial sports moments in history.

On July 8, a 75-minute television special called *The Decision* aired on ESPN and drew 10 million

Some Cavaliers fans didn't react well to LeBron James announcing his departure in 2010.

OLD-SCHOOL THINKING

According to Michael Jordan, he wouldn't have made the same decision as James, because he wouldn't have wanted to play alongside his rivals. "There's no way . . . I would've ever called up Larry [Bird], called up Magic [Johnson] and said, 'Hey, look, let's get together and play on one team,'" Jordan said.[4] He added that the game had changed since his playing days.

viewers.[1] About 30 minutes into the broadcast, in a live interview with sportscaster Jim Gray, it was time for James to share his decision. Drawing audible gasps from the live crowd, he announced, "In the fall, I'm going to take my talents to South Beach and join the Miami Heat."[2]

James added that his decision would position him to play with fellow All-Stars Dwyane Wade and Chris Bosh to have a consistently winning team under general manager and Hall of Famer Pat Riley. He reiterated that Ohio would always be home to him. "If it was a perfect world, I would have loved to stay, because I've done so many great things for that team, they've done so many great things for me. But I feel like it's time to change."[3] The Cavaliers had learned James's decision just minutes before the show aired.

BETRAYAL OR BUSINESS MOVE?

The reaction to *The Decision* was swift and brutal. Videos flooded the internet showing Cavs fans lighting No. 23

jerseys on fire or ripping them to shreds. Police kept order in Cleveland, with officers guarding a downtown billboard featuring James in his Nike "Witness" campaign. A Cleveland newspaper posted a note on its website that began, "We understand your anger," warning that commenters leaving racist or vulgar comments or references to James's family would have their posting privileges suspended.[5] Meanwhile, James's statement "take my talents to South Beach" became a roundly mocked sound bite.

Vitriol poured in from management and other athletes as well. Cavs owner Dan Gilbert penned a furious open letter posted to the team's website, calling it a "cowardly betrayal" and a "shocking act of disloyalty."[6] Many were as upset with how the decision played out as a perceived self-promotional event as they were with the decision itself. Some fans saw the spectacle of *The Decision* as further proof of the Cleveland sports curse that had plagued the city for so many decades. Most critics did not acknowledge the fact

> *"Put the shoe on the other foot . . . the Cavs would have got rid of me at one point. Would my family burn down the organization? Of course not."[7]*
>
> — *LeBron James,* after **The Decision**

CHANGING ATTITUDES

In the decade since *The Decision*, some people's attitudes have shifted as they look back on James's announcement interview. Although most hold that the spectacle was misguided, they say that James was ahead of his time in utilizing the media, making the announcement on his own terms, and donating to charity. In 2018, Seerat Sohi of SBNation.com wrote, "The question . . . has morphed from why would he do that to, well, who wouldn't?"[11]

that the TV special's $6 million in earned advertising revenue was donated to charities. The Boys & Girls Clubs of America received $2.5 million.[8] These contributions and James's defenders, however, were largely drowned out by the negative reaction to the announcement.

A few months later, controversy reared up again after James sat for an interview with Soledad O'Brien of CNN. When asked by O'Brien whether he thought that race had played a role in the backlash to *The Decision*, James answered simply, "I think so, at times. There's always a race factor."[9] Although some accused James of playing "the race card," J. A. Adande of ESPN.com noted that his statement had merit: "It's a simple, fundamental truth in our society and, in particular, the NBA."[10] To illustrate the extreme words that he and other professional athletes receive, James shared several hateful tweets that had been directed at him, many featuring racist language.

James, Dwyane Wade, and Chris Bosh took part in a ceremony to welcome James and Bosh to Miami in July 2010.

VILLAIN OF SOUTH BEACH

There was one place that welcomed James with open arms—his new city of Miami. And it was time for him to get to work. "The Road to History starts now!"[12] James tweeted. Once again, all eyes were on James, this time part of a superstar trio dubbed "The Big Three," with Wade and Bosh. "They'd better flatten the earth and take no prisoners. The Heat never had more heat," wrote Mike LoPresti of *USA Today*.[13]

To begin his career with the Heat, James switched his No. 23 jersey for No. 6. Along with Bosh and Wade,

James agreed to a smaller salary than he could have earned with other teams. That allowed the Heat to sign all three players while remaining under the NBA's salary cap. But to James's frustration, the Heat experienced growing pains as the team figured out how to best utilize its stars and supporting cast. Miami started the season with a 9–8 record. It was "too much sizzle, and not enough steak," according to one pundit, noting that star power wasn't enough to win games.[14] After regrouping in a players-only meeting, the Heat bounced back and finished with a 58–24 regular-season record.

Roundly labeled as spoiled and egocentric, James found himself topping such lists as "most hated player" and "most disliked male athlete." For a time, James embraced the role of a villain. Rather than play with his trademark sense of fun and congeniality, he acted sullen, a lonely figure that seemed to thrive off the energy of

James said he didn't mind playing the role of a villain when he joined the Heat.

booing crowds rather than chemistry with his teammates. "I might as well wear the black hat," he later remembered thinking.[16] With the jeers and words of his critics loud in his ears, he let the negative attention affect his whole game. "It basically turned me into somebody I wasn't. . . . I started to play the game of basketball . . . at a mind state that I've never played at before . . . angry."[17]

James received a rude welcome when he and the Heat played in Cleveland on December 2, 2010.

One date stood out on the schedule: December 2, 2010, the night the Heat would face the Cavaliers in Cleveland. James's only thought was to dominate. The night of the game, the Cleveland crowd was predictably unwelcoming, holding signs splashed with accusations like "Traitor" and booing every time their former MVP touched the ball. The Heat won 118–90. Reflecting on the game almost a decade later, James stated, "I will never forget that day."[18]

In the playoffs, the Heat rolled over the Philadelphia 76ers, Boston Celtics, and Chicago Bulls in five games each

to face the Dallas Mavericks in the 2011 Finals. But James's hope for a championship was denied again, as Miami fell four games to two. James was criticized for faltering toward the finish and pulling late-game "vanishing acts" in which his scoring went quiet. While Miami made its playoff run, James's stumbling hometown Cavaliers went a dismal 19–63, their worst record in eight years. King James's detractors, however, were consoled by one fact— even with his flashy new team and villain persona, James still had not won an NBA championship.

WE ARE THE
CHAMPIONS

For James, the pressure to win a championship intensified during the 2011–12 season. In a season shortened by a labor dispute between the players and owners, the Heat went 46–20, with James averaging 27.1 points, 7.9 rebounds, and 6.2 assists per game. He won his third NBA MVP Award and had returned to his preferred style of play, abandoning the villain act he'd adopted during his first season in Miami. "I play the game fun, joyful, and I let my game do all of the talking and I got away from that. That's what I lost last year," he said.[1]

In the first round of the 2012 playoffs, the Heat topped the New York Knicks in five games. Next up: the Indiana Pacers. Even with Chris Bosh out temporarily with an injury, the Heat took the series four games to two.

CHAPTER SEVEN

LeBron James finally won his coveted NBA title in 2012.

THE BIG THREE

The superstar trio of James, Dwyane Wade, and Chris Bosh had been NBA rookies together, part of the Draft Class of 2003. They all became standouts on their respective teams. James and Wade had discussed their playing futures since at least 2006, when they both decided to sign three-year extension deals to keep their options open, knowing they would become free agents at the same time.[2]

Miami next faced James's old nemesis, the Boston Celtics, who featured a formidable trio of their own in Kevin Garnett, Rajon Rondo, and Paul Pierce. The series went the full seven games. James posted 45 points and 15 rebounds in Game 6 and 31 points and 12 rebounds in Game 7 as the Heat rallied to win the final two games and the series. For the third time in his career, James had led a team into the NBA Finals.

Waiting for the Heat in the 2012 Finals were the Oklahoma City Thunder, led by MVP runner-up Kevin Durant and dynamic point guard Russell Westbrook. With Miami up 2–1 in the series, James was carried off the floor at one point during Game 4, plagued by leg cramps. He returned a few minutes later, drilling a 3-pointer to put the Heat ahead for good. With a 121–106 win in Game 5, Miami clinched the NBA Championship. James contributed to the clinching victory with a triple-double of 26 points, 11 rebounds, and 13 assists. The performance helped earn him the Finals MVP award.

It was time to celebrate. Confetti swirled inside American Airlines Arena as Queen's "We Are the Champions" played. In championship T-shirt and hat, James held the Larry O'Brien NBA Championship Trophy high. Finally, he had achieved the title in what he called "the greatest moment of my life," adding, "You know, I dreamed about this opportunity and this moment for a long time, including last night, including today. . . . My dream has become a reality now; it's the best feeling I ever had."[3] Now that James had tasted championship glory, he wasn't going to be satisfied with less.

OFF THE COURT

By this time, James's net worth was estimated to be $110 million, and he was the fourth-highest paid athlete in the world, making $53 million per year. In addition to Nike, his many endorsements included Coca-Cola, McDonald's, and Samsung. He had struck a much-publicized deal in 2011 with Fenway Sports Group, which made him a minority owner in British soccer club Liverpool FC. James's business savvy was complimented by his new friend, billionaire Warren Buffet, who said, "He's smart about financial matters. It's amazing to me the maturity

James shows off his new LeBron 12 shoes at Nike headquarters in 2014.

he exhibits. I know that if I had been famous at that age, I would have had trouble keeping my feet on the ground."[4]

James's family was also growing. In 2011, he had proposed to longtime girlfriend Savannah Brinson at a New Year's Eve party in Miami, presenting her with a five-carat diamond ring worth $300,000. On September 14, 2013, LeBron and Savannah were married in San Diego, California, in a celebrity-filled event that reportedly included a performance by the couple's friends Beyoncé and Jay-Z. On October 22 of the following year, LeBron and Savannah welcomed daughter Zhuri James, their third child.

Being a father prompted James to speak out further against social injustice, and his popular social media accounts amplified his voice. In March 2012, he took to Twitter to condemn the killing of African American teenager Trayvon Martin in Florida. James, Wade, and their Heat teammates posed for a photo in hooded sweatshirts, their faces hidden, to protest the shooting of Martin, who had been wearing a hoodie when he was shot by a suspicious neighbor. James tweeted the photo with the hashtags "#WeAreTrayvonMartin #Hoodies #Stereotyped #WeWantJustice."[5]

The MVP continued his charitable work, never forgetting his hometown even while playing in Miami. In 2011, he launched his foundation's Wheels for Education program, which kicked off with a bike ride through Akron.

ESPY WINNER

In addition to cohosting the ESPYs, James has won his fair share. In 2013, he won three, including male athlete of the year, beating out other contenders such as baseball player Miguel Cabrera, football player Adrian Peterson, and swimmer Michael Phelps. Game 6 of the 2013 NBA Finals between the Miami Heat and the San Antonio Spurs received the ESPY for best game. As of 2018, James had won the ESPY for best NBA player seven times (2007, 2009, 2012, 2013, 2016, 2017, and 2018).

In 2013, he donated $1 million to St. V for a new basketball gym (renamed the LeBron James Arena) before supplying new Nike uniforms for the school's football team.

BUILDING MOMENTUM

During the 2012 Summer Olympics in London, James took home his second gold medal with the USA men's basketball team. In the regular NBA season, the Heat posted a record of 66–16 that included a 27-game winning streak. In December, *Sports Illustrated* named James its Sportsperson of the Year. On January 16, 2013, he scored his 20,000th point. At 28 years and 17 days old, he was the youngest player in NBA history to do so, surpassing the previous record holder Kobe Bryant (who had been 29 years and 122 days old when he did it ten years earlier).

In the 2013 playoffs, the Heat lost just one game in defeating the Milwaukee Bucks and Chicago Bulls in the first two rounds. The Indiana Pacers

TAKING TO TWITTER

In 2014, the police killing of African American teen Michael Brown in Ferguson, Missouri, rocked the country, eliciting protests and riots. It also prompted James to speak up, saying that he felt emotionally connected because of his own two sons. He felt that it was his duty as a role model to say something. He tweeted: "As a society how do we do better and stop things like this happening time after time!! I'm so sorry to these families. Violence is not the answer people. Retaliation isn't the solution as well. #PrayersUpToTheFamilies #WeHaveToDoBetter."[6]

put up a better fight in the Eastern Conference Finals, but the Cavaliers prevailed in seven games to reach the NBA Finals for the third year in a row. This time they faced the San Antonio Spurs, which still featured Tim Duncan, Tony Parker, and Manu Ginóbili from the team that knocked off James's Cavaliers in 2007. Since 1999 the Spurs had been to the NBA Finals four times and won four titles.

The Heat needed every ounce of skill and determination in the clash of titan teams that went the full seven games. In Game 7, LeBron recorded 37 points and 12 rebounds, while Wade had 23 points and 10 rebounds in the Heat victory. "They played Hall of Fame basketball tonight," said Spurs coach Gregg Popovich.[7] The Heat were back-to-back NBA Champions, and LeBron earned his fourth league MVP award.

WHEELS FOR EDUCATION

In 2011, the LeBron James Family Foundation launched its Wheels for Education program in partnership with Akron Public Schools. On the program's one-year anniversary, James wrote an open letter to the local paper explaining that the program focused on mentoring, tutoring, and supporting third graders until they graduated from high school. James credited his own mentors and the Akron community for giving him opportunities and ensuring he graduated from high school. He said that he and the students had made a promise to each other to remain committed to their education. "I wear a bracelet that says 'I promise,' as a reminder to not let the kids down, on and off the court."[8]

With their NBA reign firmly secured, the Heat looked for a three-peat the following year. After a 54–28 regular season, they cruised through the Eastern Conference playoffs to earn an NBA Finals rematch with the Spurs. This time, the Heat fell in five games, hobbled by San Antonio's execution of practically flawless basketball. The loss in the Finals would mark the end of an era. Soon after, in 2014, James made an important announcement: He was heading home.

SHOW TIME

Founded by James and business partner Maverick Carter, SpringHill Entertainment media company had its first successful production with a basketball dramedy that premiered in 2014. *Survivor's Remorse* aired on Starz and concluded its four-season run in 2017. James and Maverick were both listed as executive producers.

LeBron congratulates his teammates after beating the Pacers in 2013.

"I'M COMING HOME"

When James announced his decision to return to the Cavaliers before the 2014–15 season, it lacked the drama of his more infamous 2010 decision. Rather than stage a television event, he worked with sports journalist Lee Jenkins to publish a letter of explanation in *Sports Illustrated*. Clearly, the move was not born out of a selfish desire to play with a better team—without him, the Cavs had failed miserably, going 97–215 during James's four seasons in Miami. Rather, some people compared James's Miami experience to a "leaving the nest" type of coming of age. Now, he wanted to bring a championship home.

"In Northeast Ohio, nothing is given," his essay concluded. "Everything is earned. You work for what you have. I'm ready to accept the challenge. I'm coming home." Most Cleveland fans welcomed him back with open arms, the rocky

Cavaliers fans rejoiced in the summer of 2014 when James announced he was coming back to Cleveland.

past seemingly forgotten or forgiven. The front page of the Cleveland newspaper featured James with the bold word "Home."[1] Back in Miami, some fans burned their Heat jerseys, while others vandalized a mural featuring James's image.

The Cavs team had some rebuilding to do to support its superstar. Wheeling and dealing from the Cavs' front office procured All-Star Kevin Love, who joined James and Kyrie Irving to complete Cleveland's new Big Three. The team ground through the first season together, going 53–29 to reach the playoffs. They swept the Celtics, slipped past the Chicago Bulls in six games, and wiped out the Atlanta Hawks in four straight to reach the 2015 NBA Finals.

There they faced the rapidly rising Golden State Warriors,

> *"My relationship with Northeast Ohio is bigger than basketball. People there have seen me grow up. I sometimes feel like I'm their son."*[2]
> — LeBron James, 2014

INKED UP

James has steadily added tattoos since he was a teenager. In high school, he had to cover his ink during games to follow school policy. One of his first tattoos came after his appearance on the *Sports Illustrated* cover: "Chosen1" across his back. Other notable tattoos include a lion head and the numbers "303" (Akron's area code) on his right arm. He also has words such as "Witness" (referencing a Nike ad campaign), "Gifted Child," "Beast," and "Hold My Own."[3] References to his family appear in tattoo form, too.

Kevin Love, left, and Kyrie Irving, right, joined James to form a new Big Three with the Cavs.

led by the long-range shooting of the "Splash Brothers," Stephen Curry and Klay Thompson. With Irving and Love both lost to injuries, James put on monster performances, averaging 35.8 points, 13.3 rebounds, and 8.8 assists in the series. But it wasn't enough to overtake the Warriors, who captured the series in six games. "Tried as much as

SILVER SCREEN

In 2015, James appeared on the big screen with a role in the comedy film *Trainwreck*, starring Amy Schumer and Bill Hader. His performance and comedic timing were praised by critics, with *Variety* calling his delivery "deadpan perfection," and the *New York Times* labeling him a "surprisingly limber comic presence."[5]

we could to make up for those guys, but that's a lot of talent sitting in suits," LeBron said afterward.[4]

BRINGING HOME THE HARDWARE

The next season, the Cavs seemed to have found a better groove. With a midseason coaching change that placed Tyronn Lue as head coach, the Cavs swept the Detroit Pistons and the Hawks and then knocked off the Toronto Raptors in six games to land back in the Finals.

Once again, they faced the Golden State Warriors for a shot at redemption. The Cavs fought back after trailing 3–1 to a Warriors team whose star Curry had suffered injuries throughout the postseason. In a physical Game 4, James stepped over the Warriors' Draymond Green after a tangle on the floor. Seeing it as a sign of disrespect, Green took a swing at James, leading to a scuffle that resulted in a one-game suspension for Green. The hard-fought series went the full seven games. When the game clock hit zero to conclude Game 7, the Cavs stood victorious, 93–89. For the first time ever, the Cleveland Cavaliers were

NBA champions. An emotional James, the Finals MVP, knew how much the title meant to not only him but also his city. "Cleveland, this is for you," he said.[6]

For his efforts, James was named Sportsperson of the Year by *Sports Illustrated*. Referring to the 2016 Finals, the magazine said, "Considering the opponent, the deficit, and the stakes—for himself and his region, eternally entwined—it is hard to find a more prodigious championship performance in sports history, much less basketball history."[7]

In August, James signed a three-year, $100 million extension with the Cavs. He had high hopes to continue the championship success with his hometown team. Unfortunately for LeBron and the Cavs, the championship remained out of reach for the following two seasons, despite consecutive Finals appearances. In the 2016–17 season, the Cavs met the Warriors in the Finals for the third straight year, but they lost in five games. The next season, the Cavs were swept by the Spurs.

THE BLOCK

Late in Game 7 of the 2016 Finals, James made one of the most famous defensive plays in NBA history. Chasing down Golden State's Andre Iguodala on a fast break, James leaped and slapped the ball out of Iguodala's hands before he could reach the rim for a layup. The ball struck the backboard and landed back in the Cavs' hands. Cleveland went on to win the game and the series.

James rejoices with his teammates after beating the Golden State Warriors in Game 7 of the 2016 NBA Finals.

MAKING WAVES

Throughout his return stint in Cleveland, James was expanding his influence—and his earnings. In June 2014, James made his highest appearance yet on the annual *Forbes* list of the world's top-paid athletes, coming in third behind boxer Floyd Mayweather Jr. and soccer star Cristiano Ronaldo. James had earned a reported $72.3 million, with $53 million of it coming from endorsements.[8] In 2015, he was elected vice president of the NBA's players' union. The same year, he signed a historic lifetime endorsement contract with Nike. Although terms were kept secret, the amount has since been reported to be over $1 billion.[9]

By 2016, James's reported net worth was $275 million.[10] That year, he was the highest-paid player in the NBA at $71 million.[11] James was well known for his charitable giving, announcing the previous year that the LeBron James Family Foundation would fund more than 1,100 full college scholarships for Akron children through its "I Promise" program.[12]

Being in the headlines was nothing new for James. But beginning in 2016, it seemed as though his name was in the news just as often for his off-court activities as for his

AN INFLUENCER

In 2005, James was surprised to find himself included in the *TIME* 100, the magazine's annual list of 100 most influential people in the world. As of 2018, he had been on the list three times (2005, 2013, 2017), joining other three-timers such as political leader Nelson Mandela, activist Malala Yousafzai, former first lady Michelle Obama, and actor Brad Pitt. MLB player Derek Jeter wrote the 2013 entry about James, commenting on his dedication to giving back to Akron and Ohio. "LeBron cares deeply about these places, and that says a lot about him."[13]

on-court performances. He threw his support behind Hillary Clinton in the 2016 presidential election. In an opening statement at the 2016 ESPY Awards, he joined with Carmelo Anthony, Chris Paul, and Dwyane Wade to call for an end to injustice and racial violence. "Let's use this moment as a call to action for all professional athletes to educate ourselves," James said. "Speak up. Use our influence. And renounce all violence."[14] James continued speaking up, soon finding himself at odds with conservative critics—including the newest president of the United States.

James's charitable efforts have long focused on improving the lives of children.

LEGACY OF
GREATNESS

Following Donald Trump's 2016 presidential election, LeBron James began making headlines with his outspoken criticism of the Republican and his controversial policies, later referring to Trump as the "so-called president." After Trump's immigration ban on various Muslim-majority countries, James said, "Diversity is what makes this country so great. We should all continue to speak up and fight for ideas that bring people together regardless of race, gender, ethnicity, religious beliefs, or any other differences. It's important that we as athletes continue to use the platform we have to speak up for what we believe in."[1] James also took part in Nike's "Equality" ad campaign.

In another instance, James defended Stephen Curry over a withdrawn invitation to the White House. He famously called Trump a "bum" in what

LeBron James made the jump to the Los Angeles Lakers in 2018.

became one of the world's most retweeted tweets of the year. "U bum @StephenCurry30 already said he ain't going! So therefore ain't no invite. Going to the White House was a great honor until you showed up!"[2] The statement was liked more than 1.4 million times and was retweeted more than 630,000 times.[3] Trump later responded by insulting James's intelligence.

By early 2018, James had more than 41 million Twitter followers, more than twice as many as any other NBA player.[4] And he was willing to speak out as he felt appropriate. Fox News host Laura Ingraham criticized him on her show for talking politics, calling his statements "barely intelligible," and concluding with advice to James and other African American athletes: "Shut up and dribble." James responded by leading his All-Star team to victory as the game's MVP before vowing he would keep speaking up. "We will definitely not shut up and dribble. . . . I mean too much to society,

James spent much of 2018 responding to criticism from people who don't agree with his political views.

too much to the youth, too much to so many kids who feel like they don't have a way out."[6] Later in the year, James and Maverick Carter produced an acclaimed three-part documentary series on Showtime called *Shut Up and Dribble.*

WEST COAST STATE OF MIND

In 2018, James opted out of his contract with the Cavs and signed a four-year contract with the Los Angeles Lakers. "In 2010, when he went to Miami, it was about championships," his agent told *Sports Illustrated*. "In 2014, when he went back to Cleveland, it was about delivering on a promise. In 2018, it was just about doing what he wants to do."[7] Cavs fans weren't nearly as upset with this move as they had been back in 2010. In November, when James returned to Cleveland to play the Cavs, the sold-out home crowd gave him several standing ovations. The same month, James scored 44 points in a game to pass Wilt Chamberlain in career points (31,420) and land in fifth place on the NBA's all-time scorers list.

WEAR AND TEAR

James has a reputation for withstanding injuries, sometimes referred to as his unique durability. Historically, he has largely avoided major injuries that would have kept him on the bench for long stretches. Still, he has suffered cramps, a sore back and knee, a broken cheekbone, and sprained ankles and wrists, among other injuries. In June 2018, he inflicted injury on himself when he punched a whiteboard in the locker room during Game 1 of the Finals. The injury to his right hand was not disclosed until after the series. "I pretty much played the last three games with a broken hand," James said.[8]

James soars for a dunk during his return to Cleveland with the Lakers in November 2018.

Although James was still exhibiting tremendous stats and leadership capabilities, questions began to surface regarding how long he would remain in the NBA as he got older. James assured fans that he had no plans to retire soon. He also mentioned the possibility of playing in the NBA at the same time as his son, who turned 14 in 2018.

King James fans were eager for what lay ahead. He and his business partners had been working for years to build an empire that would last long after his basketball career ended. For instance, his SpringHill production company (named for James's childhood apartment complex) continued producing anticipated television shows and sports documentaries. People wondered what future might lie ahead of him in show business, and reports surfaced that he would star in a *Space Jam* sequel—another way he would follow in the footsteps of his childhood idol, Michael Jordan, who starred in the original 1996 film. In 2018, he and other athletes launched a health and wellness company called Ladder.

YOUNG KING

James isn't the only basketball star in the family. Both of his sons have become known for their skills in the youth leagues. In July 2018, James's older son, LeBron Jr. ("Bronny"), made news for his impressive moves, with video of the 13-year-old's first public dunk circulating widely on the internet.

THE NEXT GENERATION

July 2018 marked a defining moment in James's life, and it had nothing to do with basketball. In a partnership between his foundation and Akron Public Schools, he opened a public school in his hometown. Called the "I Promise" School, it was focused on giving at-risk students the tools for success. The public school welcomed 240 third and fourth graders and also offered support and classes for parents and guardians. By 2022, the school planned to have first through eighth grades. If students completed the program and graduated from high school, James would pay their way to the University of Akron.

The day before the school's opening, James tweeted, "The jitters before the first day of school are real right now!!! Tomorrow is going to be one of the greatest moments (if not the greatest) of my life when we open the #IPROMISE School. This skinny kid from Akron who missed 83 days of school in the 4th grade had big dreams."[9] In late 2018, James won the off-season NBA Cares Community Assist Award for his work on the school.

CITIZENSHIP AWARD

In 2017, James won the Pro Basketball Writers' Association's annual J. Walter Kennedy Citizenship Award. The award, given to an NBA player showing "outstanding service and dedication to the community," recognized his educational work and mentorship in Akron through his foundation.[10]

Even within his endorsement deals, James was taking care to recognize his roots. In September 2018, James revealed his newest signature Nike shoe, the Harlem Fashion Row LeBron 16. He credited black women as the inspiration for the newest apparel. "African-American women are some of the strongest people on earth," he said. "As someone who has a platform, because of what I do, I thought it was important to lend that platform to a group of people that I believe are under-recognized."[11] On Instagram, James featured images of black women with the hashtag #Strongest. He highlighted his wife, mother, and daughter, as well as female athletes.

James soon kicked off his "More Than an Athlete" World Tour with Nike, meeting with fans in cities such as Shanghai, Paris, London, Berlin, Chicago, and New York City throughout the off-season. According to Nike, James's tour would focus on "empowering youth, community service, grassroots basketball activities, and basketball innovation."[12] James commented, "I think my responsibility is so much bigger than [basketball]. Who knows who's the next great leader and where they are. My job is to inspire the youth for when they have those dreams, they believe

James speaks at the opening ceremony for the "I Promise" school in Akron on July 30, 2018.

ALL-TIME SCORERS

As of the 2018–19 season, just four players led James on the all-time scorers list, and none of them were active: Michael Jordan (32,292), Kobe Bryant (33,643), Karl Malone (36,928), and Kareem Abdul-Jabbar (38,387).

that they make those dreams become true."[13]

From his early days of struggling in housing projects to his meteoric rise as a legendary basketball player who transformed the NBA, it has always been clear to James that he didn't fulfill his dreams on his own. His success came from the support of his mother, wife, and children; his mentors, coaches, and friends; the sports community; and his hometown. Even as a world-renowned athlete and wealthy philanthropist, his Twitter bio stated proudly, "EST. AKRON – ST.V/M Class of '03."[14] No matter where his fame took him, the town in northeastern Ohio would be home. He would never forget that he was "just a kid from Akron" who had been given the opportunity to become great. To him, the measure of true greatness would be giving new generations the same chance.

"He could play on the moon. He's the biggest athlete in the universe, the most important athlete in the culture. That's not going to change, no matter."[15]
— *Maverick Carter, 2018*

James hoped to show he had plenty of game left when he joined the Lakers in 2018.

TIMELINE

1984
On December 30, LeBron James is born in Akron, Ohio.

2000
LeBron and his St. Vincent–St. Mary High School team win the Ohio high school state championship, his first of three titles.

2001
LeBron is the first sophomore selected to *USA Today*'s All-USA First Team.

2002
In February, LeBron appears on the cover of *Sports Illustrated*.

2003
In June, James is selected as first overall NBA Draft pick by the Cleveland Cavaliers; in October, he makes his regular-season NBA debut.

2004
James is named Rookie of the Year; in October, James and girlfriend Savannah Brinson welcome their first child, Lebron Jr.; James establishes the LeBron James Family Foundation.

2007
On June 14, James and Brinson's second child, Bryce Maximus, is born.

2008

James wins his first Olympic gold medal with the USA men's basketball team during the Summer Games in Beijing.

2009

James wins his first NBA Most Valuable Player (MVP) Award.

2010

In July, James announces during a live television special, *The Decision*, that he will leave Cleveland to play for the Miami Heat.

2012

James and the Miami Heat win the NBA Championship.

2013

James and the Miami Heat win their second straight NBA title; in September, James and Savannah Brinson are married.

2014

James announces that he is returning to play with the Cleveland Cavaliers; in October, James and Savannah's third child, daughter Zhuri, is born.

2018

In July, in partnership with Akron Public Schools, James's foundation opens a public school called "I Promise" School; James debuts with the Los Angeles Lakers.

ESSENTIAL FACTS

FULL NAME
LeBron Raymone James Sr.

DATE OF BIRTH
December 30, 1984

PLACE OF BIRTH
Akron, Ohio

MOTHER
Gloria James

SPOUSE
Savannah Brinson (September 14, 2013–)

CHILDREN
LeBron James Jr.
Bryce Maximus James
Zhuri Nova James

EDUCATION
St. Vincent–St. Mary High School ("St. V"), Class of 2003

CAREER HIGHLIGHTS

- NBA Championships: 3 (2012 and 2013: Miami Heat; 2016: Cleveland Cavaliers)

- No. 1 Overall Draft Pick: 2003 (Cleveland Cavaliers)

- Rookie of the Year, 2004

- NBA Most Valuable Player (MVP): 4 (2009, 2010, 2012, 2013)

- NBA All-Star MVP: 3 (2006, 2008, 2018)

- NBA Finals MVP: 3 (2012, 2013, 2016)

- Olympics: 3 (2004: Bronze; 2008: Gold; 2012: Gold)

- *Sports Illustrated* Sportsperson of the Year: 2 (2012, 2016)

- J. Walter Kennedy Citizenship Award: 2017

- LeBron James Family Foundation, established 2004

CONFLICTS

James faced pressure and heavy scrutiny early in his life due to his quick rise to fame. He was criticized for leaving his hometown to chase a championship in Miami, especially for the way he did it, choosing to announce his decision on a live television show. He also freely shares his political views, which often conflict with those of sports fans or the media.

QUOTE

"I think my responsibility is so much bigger than [basketball]. Who knows who's the next great leader and where they are. My job is to inspire the youth for when they have those dreams, they believe that they make those dreams become true."

— *LeBron James*

GLOSSARY

Amateur Athletic Union (AAU)
A sports organization with a mission dedicated to the promotion and development of amateur athletes.

diversity
The inclusion of different types of people (of different races, genders, sexual orientations, disability statuses, and cultures) in an organization.

endorsement
When a person receives money to use and talk about a specific product.

food stamps
Government vouchers exchanged for food; meant to assist low-income households.

genocide
The deliberate mass murder of a group of people.

holding company
A company that buys and controls shares of other companies.

hype
Excitement; publicity.

minority
A person or group different from most others, usually because of race, religion, education level, or income.

monologue
A long speech made by one person.

philanthropist
Someone of wealth who donates money and time to improve the lives of others.

recession

A period of negative economic growth and, usually, low demand for goods and high unemployment.

revenue

Income, especially of a company or organization and of a substantial nature.

scalping

Reselling tickets, often for more than their value.

stereotype

To use a widely held but oversimplified idea about a particular type of person or thing.

union

An organized association of workers, often in a trade or profession, formed to protect and further their rights and interests.

welfare

Financial support provided by the government to people in need.

SELECTED BIBLIOGRAPHY

Freedman, Lew. *LeBron James: A Biography*. Westport, Conn.: Greenwood, 2008.

James, LeBron, and Buzz Bissinger. *Shooting Stars*. New York: Penguin, 2009.

Lloyd, Jason. *The Blueprint: LeBron James, Cleveland's Deliverance, and the Making of the Modern NBA*. New York: Dutton, 2017.

Pluto, Terry, and Brian Windhorst. *The Franchise: LeBron James and the Remaking of the Cleveland Cavaliers*. Cleveland: Gray & Company, 2007.

FURTHER READINGS

Bodden, Valerie. *LeBron James: Champion Basketball Star*. Abdo, 2014.

Gitlin, Marty. *LeBron James*. Abdo, 2017.

ONLINE RESOURCES

To learn more about LeBron James, please visit **abdobooklinks.com** or scan this QR code. These links are routinely monitored and updated to provide the most current information available.

MORE INFORMATION

For more information on this subject, contact or visit the following organizations:

CLEVELAND CAVALIERS

Quicken Loans Arena
1 Center Court
Cleveland, OH 44115
nba.com/cavaliers
216-420-2000

LeBron James spent the majority of his NBA career playing for his hometown team.

LEBRON JAMES FAMILY FOUNDATION

lebronjamesfamilyfoundation.org

The foundation web page is the main informational center for James's charitable programs.

SMITHSONIAN NATIONAL MUSEUM OF AFRICAN AMERICAN HISTORY AND CULTURE

1400 Constitution Avenue NW
Washington, DC 20560
nmaahc.si.edu
844-750-3012

James's "Equality" sneakers are displayed at the newest Smithsonian museum.

SOURCE NOTES

CHAPTER 1. WELCOME TO JAMESTOWN

1. Pred21. "2003 NBA Draft." *YouTube*, 14 June 2013, youtube.com. Accessed 4 Mar. 2019.

2. "2003 NBA Draft."

3. "Cleveland Cavaliers Choose LeBron James with No. 1 Pick in 2003." *Cleveland*, 27 June 2013, cleveland.com. Accessed 4 Mar. 2019.

4. Marc Stein. "Cleveland Is Officially Jamestown Now." *ESPN*, 27 June 2003, espn.com. Accessed 4 Mar. 2019.

CHAPTER 2. STRUGGLES AND SUCCESSES

1. David Murphy. "LeBron James Writes Heartfelt Tribute to His Mother." *Bleacher Report*, 13 Jan. 2014, bleacherreport.com. Accessed 4 Mar. 2019.

2. Lew Freedman. *LeBron James: A Biography*. Greenwood, 2008. 6.

3. LeBron James. *Shooting Stars*. Penguin, 2009. 13.

4. Eli Saslow. "Lost Stories of LeBron, Part 1." *ESPN*, 17 Oct. 2013, espn.com. Accessed 4 Mar. 2019.

5. Freedman, *LeBron James: A Biography*, 4.

6. Saslow, "Lost Stories of LeBron, Part 1."

7. Saslow, "Lost Stories of LeBron, Part 1."

8. Sean Highkin. "LeBron James Posts Message Thanking His Dad for Not Being in His Life." *USA Today*, 20 Feb. 2014, ftw.usatoday.com. Accessed 4 Mar. 2019.

9. Saslow, "Lost Stories of LeBron, Part 1."

10. Tim Nudd. "LeBron James, Son of a Single Mother, Is at Ease with Fatherhood," *People*, 17 Aug. 2010, people.com. Accessed 4 Mar. 2019.

11. Terry Pluto. *LeBron James: The Making of an MVP*. Gray & Company, 2009. 16.

12. Dave McMenamin. "LeBron James Considered Michael Jordan 'Godly,' Prepares to Pass Bulls Great in Scoring." *ESPN*, 15 Dec. 2018, espn.com. Accessed 4 Mar. 2019.

CHAPTER 3. A SHOOTING STAR

1. Terry Pluto. *LeBron James: The Making of an MVP*. Gray & Company, 2009. 17.

2. David Lee Morgan. *LeBron James: The Rise of a Star*. Gray & Company, 2003. 47.

3. LeBron James. *Shooting Stars*. Penguin, 2009. 74.

4. Pluto, *LeBron James: The Making of an MVP*, 51.

5. James, *Shooting Stars*, 111.

6. James, *Shooting Stars*, 116.

7. James, *Shooting Stars*, 47.

8. John Ryan. "LeBron James Recounts His High School Daze." *Mercury News*, 23 July 2009, mercurynews.com. Accessed 4 Mar. 2019.

9. Morgan, *LeBron James: The Rise of a Star*, 13.

CHAPTER 4. THE BIG TIME

1. Mike Wise. "Basketball; LeBron James Is Ruled Ineligible after Taking Gifts." *New York Times*, 1 Feb. 2003, nytimes.com. Accessed 4 Mar. 2019.

2. Jack McCallum. "SI Vault: You Gotta Carry That Weight: LeBron James Enters the NBA." *Sports Illustrated*, 6 July 2015, si.com. Accessed 4 Mar. 2019.

3. Brian Windhorst. "Decade Since LeBron First Shook NBA." *ESPN*, 29 Oct. 2013, espn.com. Accessed 4 Mar. 2019.

4. @Nike. "Just a Small-Town Kid with Big-City Dreams." *Twitter*, 20 Oct. 2018, twitter.com. Accessed 4 Mar. 2019.

5. Windhorst, "Decade Since LeBron First Shook NBA."

6. "LeBron James Interview." *Inside Hoops*, 4 Jan. 2004, insidehoops.com. Accessed 8 Mar. 2019.

7. Thomas Neumann. "Twelve Things You Need to Know on the 12th Anniversary of Lebron James' NBA Debut." *ESPN*, 29 Oct. 2015, espn.com. Accessed 4 Mar. 2019.

8. "LeBron James." *Basketball Reference*, n.d., basketball-reference.com. Accessed 8 Mar. 2019.

9. Lew Freedman. *LeBron James: A Biography*. Greenwood, 2008. 87.

10. Marc Stein. "Cleveland Is Officially Jamestown Now." *ESPN*, 27 June 2003, espn.com. Accessed 4 Mar. 2019.

CHAPTER 5. THE PLAYOFFS, FINALLY

1. William C. Rhoden. "For Maverick Carter, Running King James' Empire Was Always the Game Plan." *Undefeated*, 25 May 2018, theundefeated.com. Accessed 4 Mar. 2019.

2. "Top Moments: LeBron James Dominates Pistons En Route to Finals." *NBA*, n.d., nba.com. Accessed 4 Mar. 2019.

3. Sekou Smith. "Decade of Dominance: LeBron James's First Finals Run in Cleveland." *NBA*, 29 May 2017, nba.com. Accessed 8 Mar. 2019.

4. "Can LeBron Save Darfur?" *Chicago Tribune*, 17 June 2007, chicagotribune.com. Accessed 8 Mar. 2019.

5. Tom Withers. "LeBron, Girlfriend Welcome Their 2nd Son." *Washington Post*, 14 June 2007, washingtonpost.com. Accessed 4 Mar. 2019.

6. Philip Sherwell. "Race Row over 'King Kong' Vogue Cover." *Telegraph*, 30 Mar. 2009, telegraph.co.uk. Accessed 4 Mar. 2019.

7. "Ouster Enough? No Fine for LeBron." *ESPN*, 1 June 2009, espn.com. Accessed 4 Mar. 2019.

8. Brian Windhorst. "Decade Since LeBron First Shook NBA." *ESPN*, 29 Oct. 2013, espn.com. Accessed 4 Mar. 2019.

9. @KingJames. "Hello World, the Real King James Is in the Building 'Finally.'" *Twitter*, 6 July 2010, twitter.com. Accessed 4 Mar. 2019.

10. Ben Parr. "LeBron James Surpasses 150,000 Twitter Followers in 7 Hours." *Mashable*, 6 July 2010, mashable.com. Accessed 4 Mar. 2019.

CHAPTER 6. THE DECISION

1. "Would You Pay $500K to Go to LeBron James' Birthday Party?" *CNN*, 24 Dec. 2010, cnn.com. Accessed 4 Mar. 2019.

2. Henry Abbott. "LeBron James' Decision: The Transcript." *ESPN*, 8 July 2010, espn.com. Accessed 4 Mar. 2019.

3. Abbott, "LeBron James' Decision."

4. "Jordan Wouldn't Have Called Magic, Bird." *ESPN*, 19 July 2019, espn.com. Accessed 4 Mar. 2019.

5. Brian Windhorst. "LeGone: LeBron James Announces He's Leaving Cleveland Cavaliers for Miami Heat." *Cleveland*, 9 July 2010, cleveland.com. Accessed 4 Mar. 2019.

6. "Letter from Cavs Owner Dan Gilbert." *ESPN*, 13 Dec. 2010, espn.com. Accessed 4 Mar. 2019.

7. Henry Abbott. "LeBron James' Post-Decision Interviews." *ESPN*, 12 July 2010, espn.com. Accessed 4 Mar. 2019.

8. "LeBron James' Decision Generated $6 Million in Ad Revenue." *Cleveland*, 12 July 2010, cleveland.com. Accessed 4 Mar. 2019.

9. Brian Windhorst. "LeBron James Shares Hateful Tweets." *ESPN*, 21 Oct. 2010, espn.com. Accessed 4 Mar. 2019.

10. Windhorst, "LeBron James Shares Hateful Tweets."

11. Seerat Sohi. "The Backlash to LeBron James' 'Decision' Feels Really Silly Now." *SB Nation*, 21 Nov. 2018, sbnation.com. Accessed 4 Mar. 2019.

12. @KingJames. "What's Up Yall. Just Landed in My New Home. Thanks to All the Fans and the Miami Organization Who Greeted Me. The Road to History Starts Now!" *Twitter*, 9 July 2010, twitter.com. Accessed 4 Mar. 2019.

13. "Reaction to LeBron James' Move to Miami." *CNN*, 9 July 2010, cnn.com. Accessed 4 Mar. 2019.

14. Oly Sandor. "Bosh, James, Wade, and Riley to Blame for the Heat's 9–8 Start." *Hoops Vibe*, 28 Nov. 2010, hoopsvibe.com. Accessed 8 Mar. 2019.

15. "Would You Pay $500K to Go to LeBron James' Birthday Party?"

16. @Uninterrupted. "'I Will Never Forget That Day, December 2nd, 2010 (Heat vs. Cavs.)'" *Twitter*, 12 Dec. 2018, twitter.com. Accessed 4 Mar. 2019.

17. Brian Windhorst. "LeBron James: No More Mr. Bad Guy." *ESPN*, 7 Dec. 2011, espn.com. Accessed 4 Mar. 2019.

18. @Uninterrupted. "'I Will Never Forget That Day, December 2nd, 2010 (Heat vs. Cavs.)'"

CHAPTER 7. WE ARE THE CHAMPIONS

1. Brian Windhorst. "LeBron James: No More Mr. Bad Guy." *ESPN*, 7 Dec. 2011, espn.com. Accessed 4 Mar. 2019.

2. Howard Beck. "Brotherhood." *Bleacher Report*, n.d., thelab.bleacherreport.com. Accessed 4 Mar. 2019.

3. Mike Wise. "NBA Finals 2012: LeBron James Is Worthy MVP, but Miami Heat Win Title as a Team." *Washington Post*, 22 June 2012, washingtonpost.com. Accessed 4 Mar. 2019.

4. DeAntae Prince. "LeBron James Earns Praise from Warren Buffett for Business Mind." *Sporting News*, 3 Nov. 2012, sportingnews.com. Accessed 4 Mar. 2019.

5. @KingJames. "#WeAreTrayvonMartin #Hoodies #Stereotyped #WeWantJustice." *Twitter*, 23 Mar. 2012, twitter.com. Accessed 4 Mar. 2019.

6. Joe Vardon. "LeBron James Tweets about Ferguson, Mo. Decision." *Cleveland*, 25 Nov. 2014, cleveland.com. Accessed 4 Mar. 2019.

7. Sekou Smith. "Decade of Dominance: LeBron James, Miami Heat Climb to Top of NBA Heap." *NBA*, 29 May 2017, nba.com. Accessed 4 Mar. 2019.

8. LeBron James. "Promise of an Education." *Ohio*, 19 Aug. 2012, ohio.com. Accessed 4 Mar. 2019.

CHAPTER 8. "I'M COMING HOME"

1. Nicki Jhabvala. "Reactions to LeBron James's Decision to Return to Cleveland." *Denver Post*, 11 July 2014, denverpost.com. Accessed 8 Mar. 2019.

2. Zach Hefland. "LeBron James Never Forgot Where He Came From and They Never Forgot Him." *Los Angeles Times*, 27 Oct. 2014, latimes.com. Accessed 4 Mar. 2019.

3. "Tattoos." *NikeLeBron.net*, n.d., nikelebron.net. Accessed 4 Mar. 2019.

4. Bob Finnan. *100 Things Cavaliers Fans Should Know & Do Before They Die*. Triumph, 2016.

5. Marissa Payne. "LeBron James Is Not a Train Wreck in 'Trainwreck,' Critics Say." *Washington Post*, 17 July 2015, washingtonpost.com. Accessed 18 Dec. 2018.

6. Brian Windhorst. *Return of the King*. Grand Central, 2017. 241.

7. Lee Jenkins. "Crowning the King: LeBron James Is Sports Illustrated's 2016 Sportsperson of the Year." *Sports Illustrated*, 1 Dec. 2016, si.com. Accessed 4 Mar. 2019.

8. "#3 LeBron James." *Forbes*, n.d., forbes.com. Accessed 4 Mar. 2019.

9. Emmett Knowlton. "LeBron James' Business Partner Confirms Lifetime Deal with Nike Is Worth over $1 Billion." *Business Insider*, 17 May 2016, businessinsider.com. Accessed 4 Mar. 2019.

10. Dana Olsen. "LeBron's Move to LA Might Mean More VC Deals for King James." *Pitch Book*, 11 July 2018, pitchbook.com. Accessed 8 Mar. 2019.

11. Kurt Badenhausen. "LeBron James Tops the NBA's Highest-Paid Players 2016." *Forbes*, 20 Jan. 2016, forbes.com. Accessed 8. Mar. 2019.

12. Hayley Byrnes. "LeBron James Will Pay for More Than 1,000 Kids to Go to College." *SB Nation*, 14 Aug. 2015, sbnation.com. Accessed 8 Mar. 2019.

13. Derek Jeter. "LeBron James." *Time*, 18 Apr. 2013, time.com. Accessed 4 Mar. 2019.

14. "The Ballad of the Banana Boat Brotherhood." *Ringer*, 4 Oct. 2016, theringer.com. Accessed 4 Mar. 2019.

CHAPTER 9. LEGACY OF GREATNESS

1. Marisa Guthrie. "LeBron James Rips Trump's Immigration Ban 'That Divides and Excludes People.'" *Hollywood Reporter*, 8 Feb. 2017, hollywoodreporter.com. Accessed 4 Mar. 2019.

2. Chris Chavez. "LeBron James 'U Bum' Tweet to Donald Trump Is the Most Retweeted Athlete Post of 2017." *Sports Illustrated*, 5 Dec. 2017, si.com. Accessed 4 Mar. 2019.

3. Chavez, "LeBron James 'U Bum' Tweet to Donald Trump."

4. Brent Ong. "LeBron Has Most Twitter Followers among NBA Players with 41 Million; Second Guy Has 17 Million." *Clutch Points*, 30 Aug. 2018, clutchpoints.com. Accessed 4 Mar. 2019.

5. Jeff Zillgitt. "LeBron James' Game-Worn Equality Sneakers on Display in Museum." *USA Today*, 14 Dec. 2018, usatoday.com. Accessed 4 Mar. 2019.

6. Emily Sullivan. "Laura Ingraham Told LeBron James to Shut Up and Dribble; He Went to the Hoop." *NPR*, 19 Feb. 2018, npr.org. Accessed 4 Mar. 2019.

7. Lee Jenkins. "Fit for the King: LeBron James and the Lakers Form Hollywood's Ultimate Marriage." *Sports Illustrated*, 11 July 2018, si.com. Accessed 4 Mar. 2019.

8. Sam Amick. "LeBron James' Injured Hand Leaves 2018 Finals Loss to Warriors with Big What-If Factor." *USA Today*, 10 June 2018, usatoday.com. Accessed 4 Mar. 2019.

9. Ben Axelrod. "LeBron James Wins Offseason NBA Cares Community Assist Award for I Promise School." *WKYC*, 25 Oct. 2018, wkyc.com. Accessed 4 Mar. 2019.

10. "Citizen/King: LeBron James Wins NBA Citizenship Award." *USA Today*, 21 May 2017, usatoday.com. Accessed 8 Mar. 2019.

11. Chris Ross. "LeBron James Says Harlem Fashion Row LeBron 16s Inspired by Black Women." *USA Today*, 5 Sept. 2018, lebronwire.usatoday.com. Accessed 4 Mar. 2019.

12. "LeBron James World Tour." *NBA*, n.d., nba.com. Accessed 4 Mar. 2019.

13. Nike. "Nike—LeBron James: More Than an Athlete World Tour." *YouTube*, 3 Dec. 2018, youtube.com. Accessed 4 Mar. 2019.

14. @KingJames. *Twitter*, n.d., twitter.com. Accessed 4 Mar. 2019.

15. William C. Rhoden. "For Maverick Carter, Running King James' Empire Was Always the Game Plan." *Undefeated*, 25 May 2018, theundefeated.com. Accessed 4 Mar. 2019.

INDEX

ABOUT THE AUTHOR

Laura K. Murray has written more than 60 nonfiction books. She lives in Minnesota, where she enjoys watching and writing about basketball but relies on memories of eighth grade for real-life playing experience.